Daddoo's Day Out

Prabhjot Kaur

AF516938

KATHA

Daddoo was a happy frog. She lived near a pond with her mother. And all day she played with her friends.

One night, she sat looking at the sky with her large eyes, thinking, how same every day is!

Suddenly an idea came to her.

"I'll go out and see the world!" she said to herself. "I'll make many, many new friends."

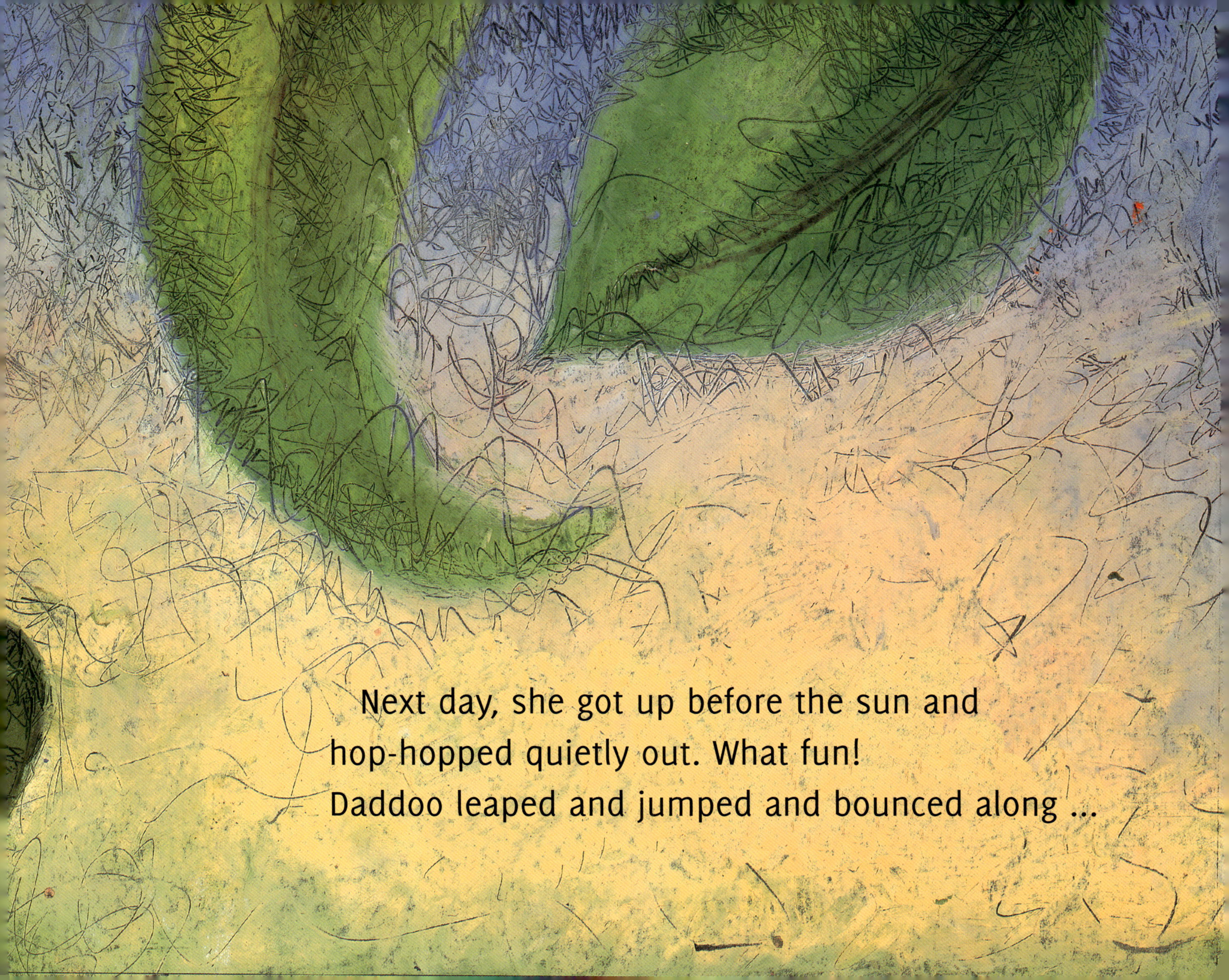

Next day, she got up before the sun and hop-hopped quietly out. What fun! Daddoo leaped and jumped and bounced along ...

Suddenly she saw a huge black snake coiled on the broken branch of a tree.

"Hello," said Daddoo.

"What are you doing all by yourself?" asked the huge black snake.

"I'm out to see the world!" said Daddoo.

"I wish I could go with you," said the snake.

Soon she came to a pond. It was much, much bigger than the nice pond where she and Ma lived.

Daddoo jumped Plop! into the water. Ahhhh! How cool it was!

Two white birds, swimming in the water, came up to say, "Hello!"

But when they opened
their mouths ...

"Ai Mai!" said Daddoo, scared.
She didn't even turn to look.
She jumped!

It was a
bigggggggggg
jump!
And ...

She landed on a hard piece of land.

"Hoosh," said Daddoo. "Safe at last."

But ...

Right in front were a pair of eyes glaring at her.

"I am Alligator!" said an alligator. "Hello!" alligator smiled. A soft, squishy smile.

"S-s-s-o-rry," stammered Daddoo.

"What for?" asked the alligator, grinning.

"Want to play?"

"Yes ... um, no, thank you!" said a frightened Daddoo. And off she went, hop-hopping away!

Slowly the sky became dark. A strong wind started to blow.

Daddoo saw a grasshopper blown by the wind. She wanted to help that tiny grasshopper before he got hurt.

But before she could do anything, the little insect disappeared.

Soon it started raining. Daddoo looked around, and saw a big mushroom. She quickly hop-hopped and hid under it.

It rained and rained and rained.

"Bye-bye little Daddoo," said the sun as it went slipping down behind the hill.

"I want to go home!" said Daddoo. But where was she? She felt very, very alone. And far from home. And Ma!

Then she saw a wisp-winged dragonfly sitting alone on a reed.

Daddoo spoke in a low voice, "Hello!"

The dragonfly fluttered his wings.

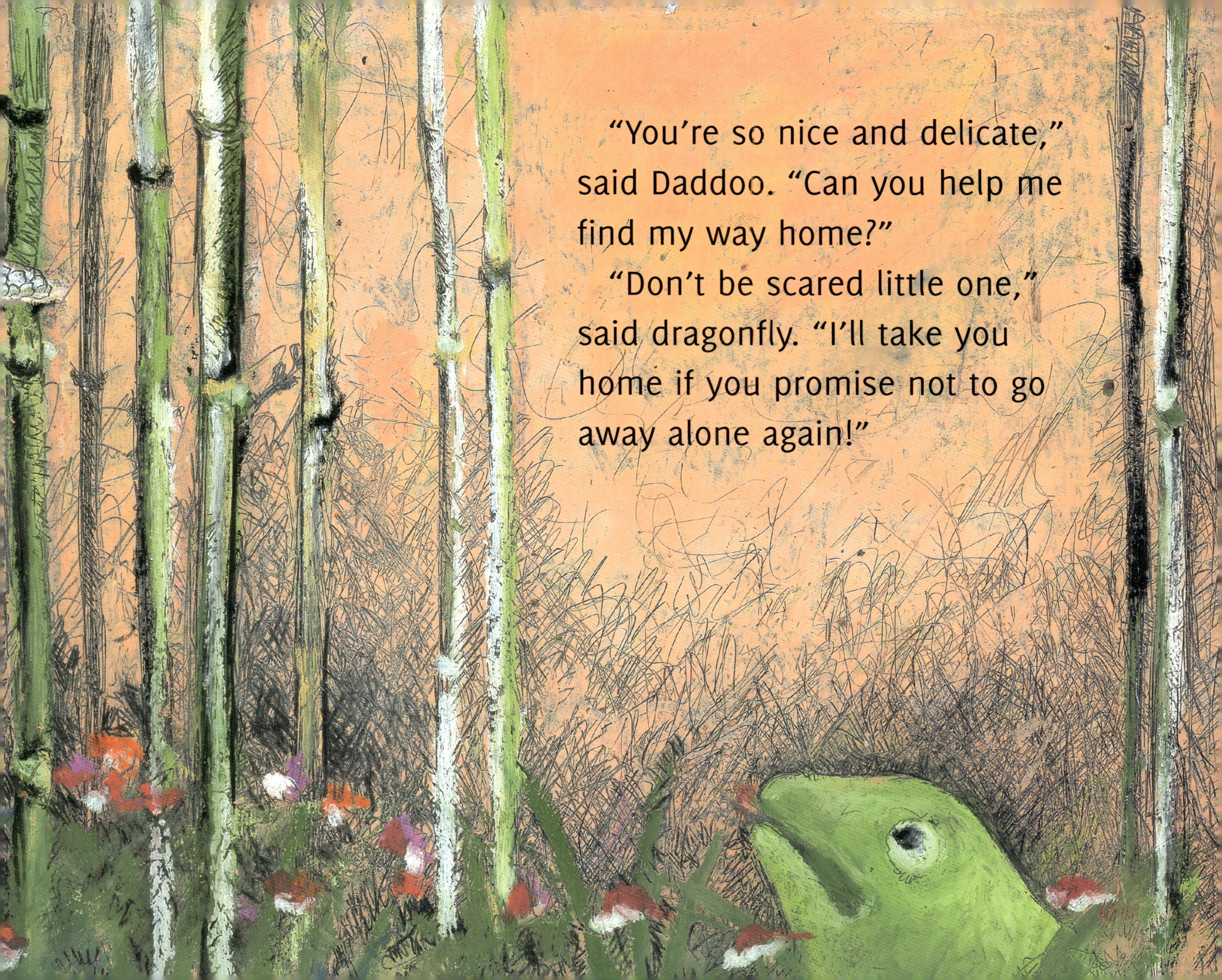

"You're so nice and delicate," said Daddoo. "Can you help me find my way home?"

"Don't be scared little one," said dragonfly. "I'll take you home if you promise not to go away alone again!"

When Daddoo reached home, it was dark and silent. But it was her pond.

Her big eyes sparkled with joy. Ma and her friends rushed towards her.

Daddoo was happy. She had come home at last!